PEZ

COLLECTIBLES

With Price Guide

RICHARD GEARY

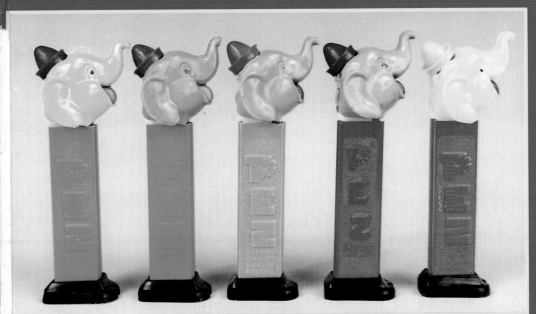

Schiffer Publishing Ltd

77 Lower Valley Road, Atglen, PA 19310

Acknowledgements

I am grateful to the following people whose guidance and friendships have made this book possible.

Thank you to Roland Austin, Chrissy Bailey, Pat Barnes, Ron Barr, Bill Clark, Jill Cohen, Earl's Restaurant, Nancy Gyumolcs, Tom Hall, Stan Luksenburg, Bill Perby, Roger Fike, the Simons family and Gordon Simpson.

Thanks to Charlie Butts and Jim Kilgour for their generosity, kindness and trust. A big thank you to Larry LaFoe for supplying computer help and providing a great newsletter.

Extra special thanks to Sue and Richie Sternfeld for all their wonderful photographs, information and constant support. Without question they have one of the nicest collections around. Their help was tremendous.

Thank you to Peter Schiffer for guiding me along and giving me so many choices.

This book is in no way affiliated with PEZ® Candy, Inc. PEZ® is a registered trademark of PEZ® Candy, Inc.

Copyright © 1994 by Richard Geary
Library of Congress Catalog Number: 94-66688

Printed in Hong Kong
ISBN: 0-88740-693-9

We are interested in hearing from authors with book ideas on related topics.

Published by Schiffer Publishing Ltd.
77 Lower Valley Road
Atglen, PA 19310
Please write for a free catalog.
This book may be purchased from the publisher.
Please include $2.95 postage.
Try your bookstore first.

Dedication

To Jason, Bryan, Melissa, Matthew and Jacob,
my terrific nephews and niece.

Contents

Introduction

Nothing has as much appeal as a PEZ® dispenser. Why, you not only get candy, but you also get a toy. By simply tilting the head back you were able to share the fun with everyone around you.

The popularity of collecting PEZ® dispensers has increased dramatically in recent years. And it's no wonder, with PEZ ®being mentioned in movies, T.V. and newspapers. There are even organized conventions that you can attend.

One of the most sought-after dispensers is the "Make-A-Face," with 18 parts you could make 158 different silly faces. But the small pieces created a hazard for kids and it was pulled from the market, making it one of the rarest dispensers around.

Licensed characters, holiday characters and more have come to life on a PEZ® dispenser. As you look through these pages you might recall which ones you owned, or you will see dispensers you didn't even know existed. But I am sure you will enjoy your trip down PEZ® lane.

History

It was over 60 years ago that a man named Eduard Haas created a compressed peppermint candy. By using the first, middle and last letters of the German word for peppermint (PfeffErminZ), the name PEZ® was derived. Then in 1952, PEZ® was brought to the United States, and the introduction of fruit flavors and character heads made their debut. Prior to the early 1950s the dispensers had no character heads, these early versions were actually made for adults and came with a thumb grip. The early dispensers are known by collectors as "Regulars."

Since the creation of character heads, there have been over 250 different types. Besides the popular T.V. and cartoon characters, there have been several of the company's own creations, one in particular is the PEZ® Pal series. These were done in part with a comic strip character named Pezi. He would change into several disguises and solve mysteries. Many other types of dispensers were also made. Collectors find it a challenge to try to get each dispenser.

"PEZ® Box". First advertised
dispenser. ca. 1940s, $400-
650

$\mathcal{C}$hapter 1: Dispensers

Dating dispensers is rather difficult. The patent number on the side of the dispenser gives a vague idea as to what time frame they were probably made. Patent number 2,620,061 (1st series) was issued in 1952, patent number 3,410,455 (2nd series) was issued in 1968, patent number 3,845,882 (3rd series) was issued in 1974, and patent number 3,942,683 (4th series) was issued in 1976. Currently the new patent number is 4,966,305 (5th series). It is important to note that the patent number and country have nothing to do with the value of the dispenser. And, there are dispensers with no patent number at all.

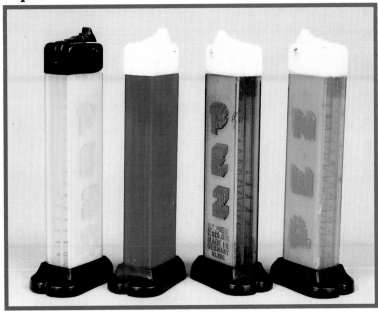

"U.S. Zone Regular". Made in Germany. ca. 1940s, $135-200

Currently, feet are now a part of the dispenser and háve been since the mid 1980s. Several dispensers are found both with and without feet, but with the same head, there is a fine line as to whether there is a difference in price, most collectors are interested in the character head, and are not concerned with the idea of having a footed or non-footed dispenser.

Unfortunately, a problem you may run into is people trimming off the feet and trying to pass them off as older dispensers. By comparing the older footless dispensers next to the newer footed ones you will notice a big difference in case sizes. Most people are honest and I don't see this as a real big problem.

Missing parts is also a problem. It is important to notice the accessories that go with each dispenser. Missing pieces decrease the value dramatically, and some parts can never be found.

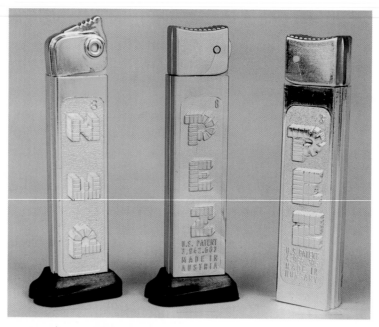

"Golden Glow" and "Silver Glow A" and "Silver Glow B". The Golden Glow was offered as a premium. $75-100, Silver Glow "A" $225-350, Silver Glow "B" $10-20

Variations of certain dispensers are becoming very popular, especially with advanced collectors. Maybe the character is a different color, or the head is a different shape or the character head has different color parts. Whatever the reason, collectors are looking for something other than the common version of that dispenser.

Because of variations, collectors have used a lettering system to identify certain mold changes of character heads. For whatever reason, if the head of the same character changes you will see a letter for each different head (A, B, C, etc.) with "A" being the earliest version.

Finally, it is important to note that with so many different dispensers being made there is unfortunately some bootleg dispensers being made, collectors need to be careful and learn their hobby before spending a lot of money. There are newsletters and collectors who are always willing to help and educate. Enjoy your hobby and have fun with it.

"Witch Regular". ca. 1950s, $1,000-1,500

"Advertising Regulars". These are very rare and popular with collectors. $300-400

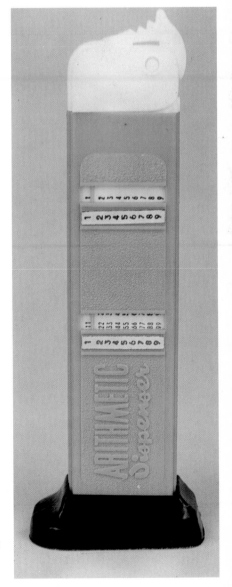

"Arithmetic Regular". This would actually multiply when the sleeve was pulled out. $175-275

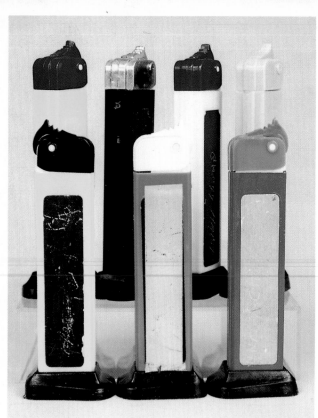

"Personalized Regular". Available as a premium. You could write your name on the side. $100-150

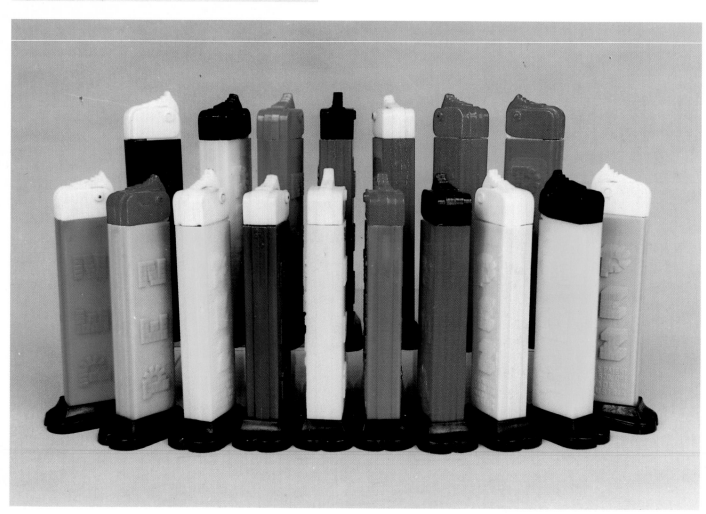

"Regulars". Early version of dispensers. $100-150

"Mickey Mouse© Die-Cut", ca. 1960s, $100-125

"Mickey Mouse© "C", "D" and "E". The "C" has a removable nose. $10-15, "D" nose is part of head. $5-10, "E" is revised version. $1-3

"Mickey Mouse© "A" and "B". "A" has a die-cut face. $40-60, "B" has a painted face. $75-100

"Pluto© "A", "B" and "C". "A" has rounded head, removable ears. $5-15, "B" flat head, removable ears. $10-20, "C" revised. $1-3

"Goofy© "C". The "C" has the nose and teeth as part of the head. $3-5,

"Goofy© "A" and "B". "A" has removable teeth. $5-15, "B" nose and teeth removable. $35-65

"Donald Duck© "A", "B" and
"Soft-Head". "A" $1-5, "B" $1-3,
Soft-Head (front right) $300-
400

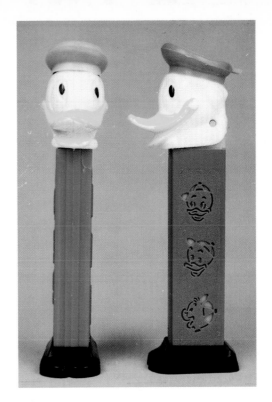

"Donald Duck© Die-Cut" ca.
1960s, $100-125

"Huey, Dewey and Louie©".
European issue. $1-5

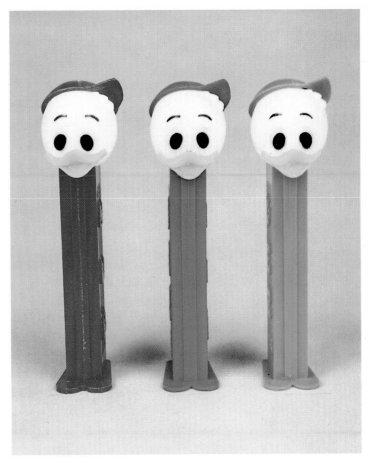

"Duck Child". Early versions of
Dewey and Louie. $15-25

"Scrooge McDuck© "A" and "B".
$5-15

"Jiminy Cricket© WDP". $25-40

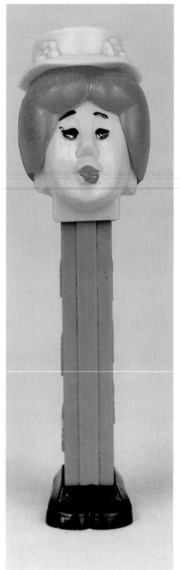

"Mary Poppins©". A very rare piece. ca. 1960s, $400-500

"Gyro Gearloose, Bouncer Beagle, Webby©". European issue. $1-5

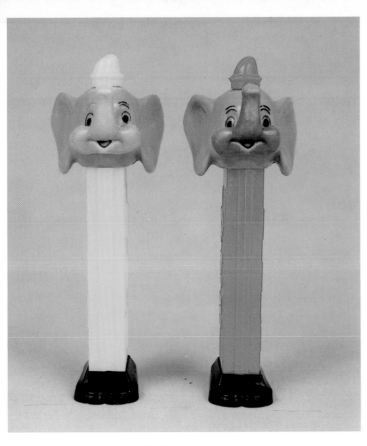

"Winnie the Pooh© WDP". $10-20

"Dumbo© WDP". Two versions, gray head $75-100, blue head $20-30

"Pinocchio© WDP". Version "A" comes in yellow or red cap. $75-100, Version "B" $25-40

"Practical Pig". The "A" version has a rounded cap. Version "B" has a crooked cap. $20-30

"Chip© WDP". $20-30

"Li'l Bad Wolf© WDP". $10-20

"Thumper© WDP". $45-65

"Baloo© WDP". Blue face $15-25, yellow face $150-200

"Dalmation Pup, Mowgli and Bambi© WDP", ca. 1980s, $15-25

"Dopey and Peter Pan© WDP". ca. 1960s, (left) $100-150, (right) $50-75

"Snow White© WDP". ca. 60s, $50-75

"Tinkerbelle© WDP". ca. 1960s, $75-125

"Captain Hook© WDP". $20-30

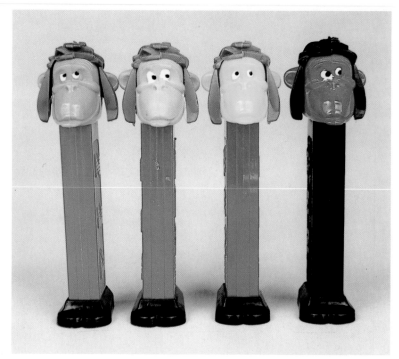

"King Louie© WDP". Brown version $10-20, yellow version $150-200, red version $150-200

"Zorro© WDP. "A" and "B", ca. 1960s, "A" $25-35, "B" $30-40, with logo $50-75

"Flinstones© H.B." (Fred,
Barney, Pebbles and Dino), $1-
3

"Garfield© UFS, Inc.",
(Garfield, Arlene and Nermal),
$1-3

"Smurfs© Peyo", (Papa,
Smurfette and Smurf), $1-5

"Muppets© Henson Assoc.,
Inc.", (Gonzo, Fozzie, Kermit
and Miss Piggy), $1-3

"Charlie Brown© UFS, Inc.",
Smiling $1-3, tongue $1-5,
frown $1-5, eyes closed $25-45

"Woodstock and Snoopy© UFS,
Inc.", $1-3

"Lucy© UFS, Inc.", $1-5, white
eyes $25-45

"Popeye© KFS, Inc.". Original,
ca. 1950s, $100-150

"Olive Oyl© KFS, Inc.", ca.
1950s, $100-150

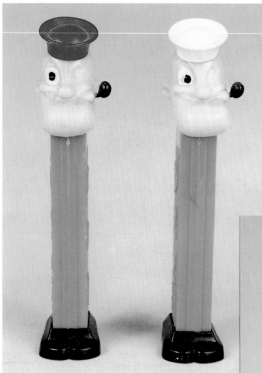

"Popeye© KFS, Inc. "C". With
pipe. ca. 1970s, $40-60

"Brutus© KFS, Inc.", ca.
1950s, $100-150

"Popeye© KFS, Inc. "B". ca.
1960s, $25-40

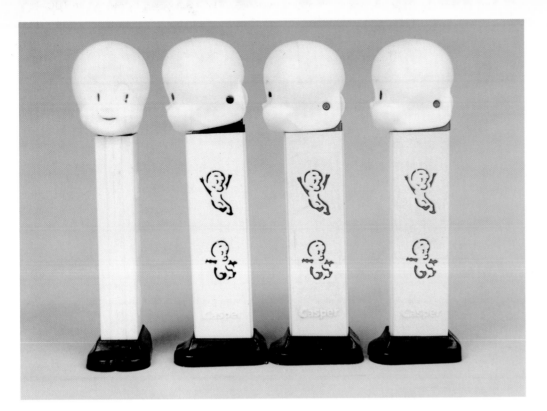

"Casper© Harvey". ca. 1960s,
$50-75, Die-cut with cutout on
the side. $100-125

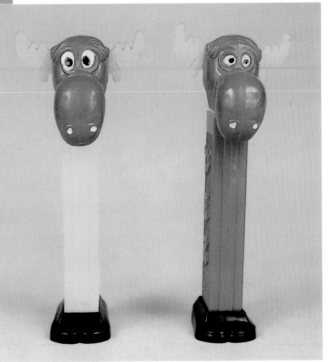

"Annie© Chicago Tribune,
Suns, Inc.". ca. 1980s, $45-65

"Bozo© CPI". ca. 1960s, $50-
75, Die-cut on side. $100-125

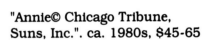

"Bullwinkle© P.A.T. Ward". ca.
1960s, $175-225

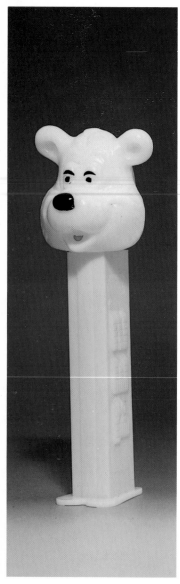

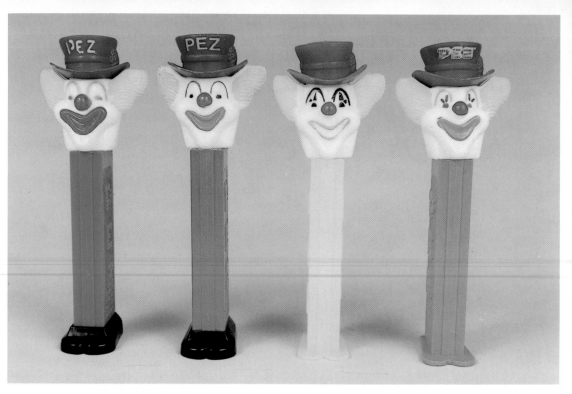

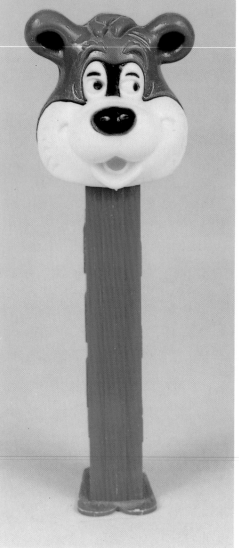

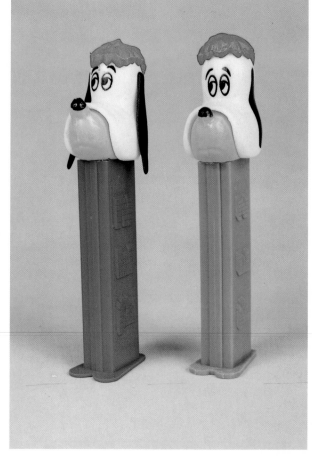

"Peter PEZ®", Older version. ca. 1970s, $50-75, Revised version. (far right) $1-5

"Droopy Dog© MGM "A" and "B"", ca. 1980s, "A" $5-10, "B" $1-5

"Icee Bear". ca. 1990s, $5-10

"Barney Bear© MGM", ca. 1980s, $25-35

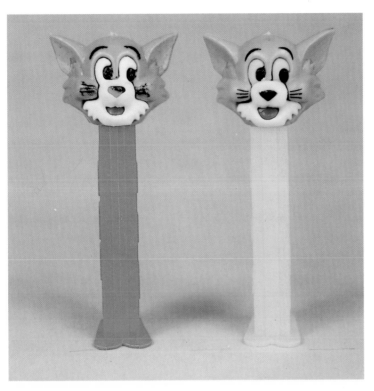

"Tom© MGM "B". ca. 1980s.
White or yellow eyes. $5-10

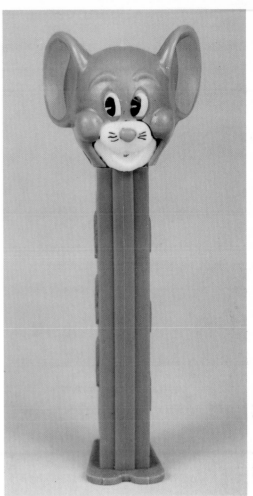

"Tuffy© MGM "A". ca. 1990s,

"Spike© MGM "A". ca. 1980s,
$10-20

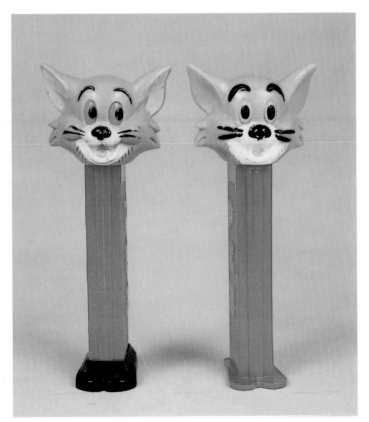

"Tom© MGM "A" and "C", ca.
1980s, "A" $10-25, "C" $1-5

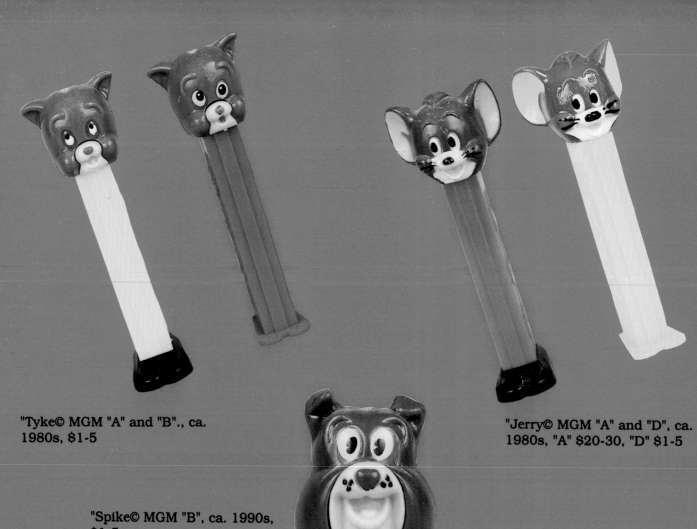

"Tyke© MGM "A" and "B"., ca. 1980s, $1-5

"Jerry© MGM "A" and "D", ca. 1980s, "A" $20-30, "D" $1-5

"Spike© MGM "B", ca. 1990s, $1-5

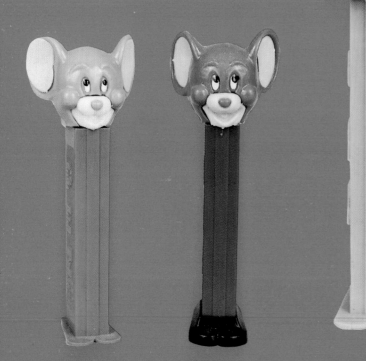

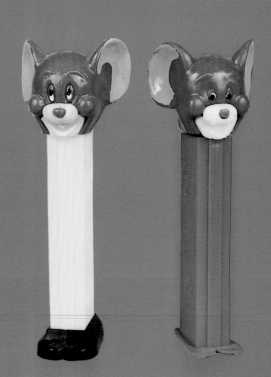

"Tuffy "B" and Jerry© MGM "C". Removable inner ears. ca. 1990s, $30-40

"Jerry© MGM "B", ca. 1990s, "B" $1-5

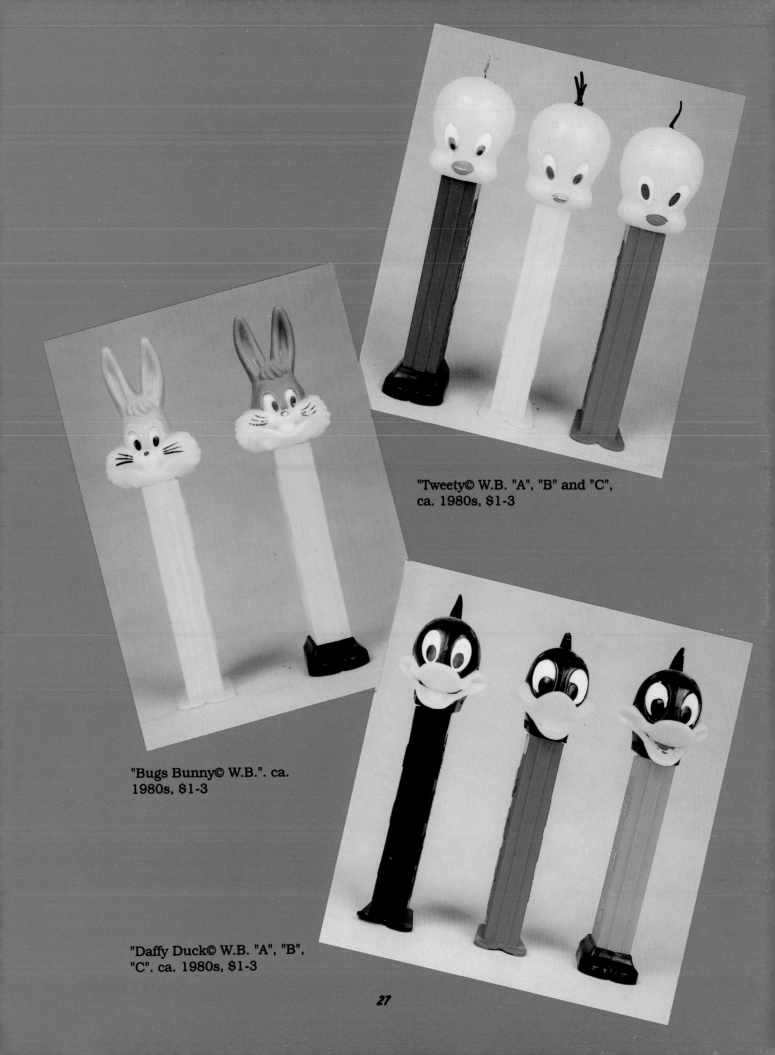

"Tweety© W.B. "A", "B" and "C",
ca. 1980s, $1-3

"Bugs Bunny© W.B.". ca.
1980s, $1-3

"Daffy Duck© W.B. "A", "B",
"C". ca. 1980s, $1-3

27

"Sylvester© W.B.", ca. 1980s,
$1-3

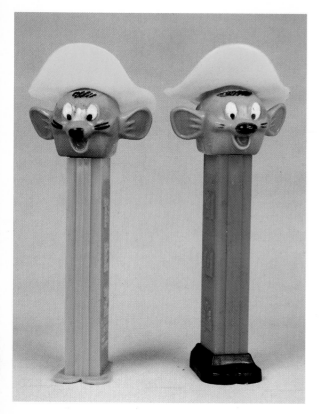

"Wile E. Coyote© W.B.", ca.
1980s, $10-20

"Speedy Gonzales© W.B.", ca.
1980s, $1-5

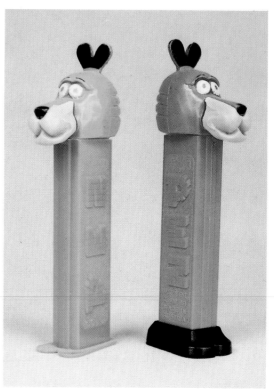

"Cool Cat© W.B.", ca. 1980s,
orange $30-40, pink $150-200

"Merlin Mouse, Henry Hawk and Petunia Pig© W.B.", ca. 1980s, Merlin Mouse $1-5, Henry Hawk $30-50, Petunia Pig $30-50

"Road Runner© W.B. "A" and "B", ca. 1980s, $1-5

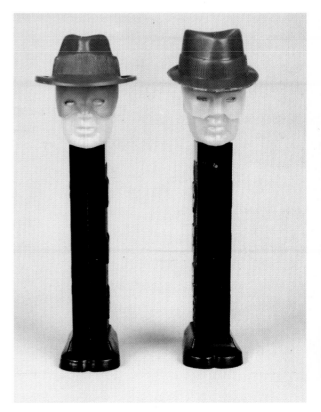

"Green Hornet© Greenway Prod.", ca 1960s, $150-200

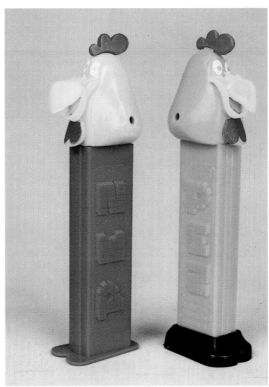

"Foghorn Leghorn© W.B.", ca. 1980s, $35-45

"Batman© D.C. Comics", ca 1980s, blue $1-3, black $75-125

"Thor© D.C. Comics", ca 1980s, $125-150

"Batman w/Cape© D.C. Comics", ca. 1960s, $125-150

"Captain America© D.C. Comics", ca. 1980s, $35-65

"Soft-Head Super Hero's",
(Wonder Woman, Penguin,
Joker, Batman, Batgirl© D.C.
Comics), ca 1970s, $75-100

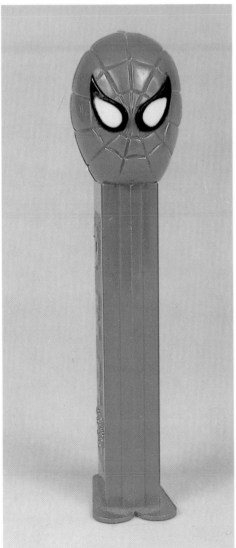

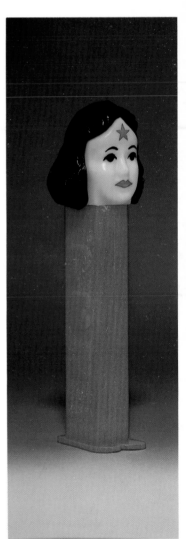

"Spiderman© D.C. Comics "A",
ca. 1970s, $3-5

"Wonder Woman© D.C. Com-
ics", ca. 1980s, $1-3

"Spiderman© D.C. Comics "B",
ca. 1990s, $1-3

"Hulk© D.C. Comics "B", ca. 1990s, $1-3

"Fishman". There is no copyright on these. ca. 1970s, $125-175

"Hulk© D.C. Comics "A", ca. 1970s, $10-15

"Wolfman, Creature from the Black Lagoon, Frankenstein© U.P.C.", ca. 1960s, $150-250

"Bride and Groom", (PEZ® Pal),
ca. 1960s. Very scarce. Groom
$150-175, Bride $500-600

"Sheriff and Policeman" (PEZ®
Pal), ca. 1960s, Policeman
$10-20, Sheriff $65-95

"Fireman" (PEZ® Pal), ca.
1960s, $10-20

"Doctor" (PEZ® Pal), ca. 1960s,
$40-60

"Nurse" (PEZ® Pal), ca. 1960s,
$40-60

"Boy" (PEZ® Pal), ca. 1970s,
blond $25-35, with feet $1-3

"Boy w/Cap" (PEZ® Pal), ca.
1960s, $20-40

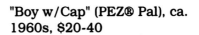

"Girl" (PEZ® Pal), ca. 1970s,
white $15-25, blond with feet
$1-3

"Mexican Boy" (PEZ® Pal), ca.
1960s, $30-50

"Pirate, Sailor and Ringmaster"
(PEZ® Pal), ca. 1960s, Pirate
$25-35, Sailor $75-90, Ringmaster $80-100

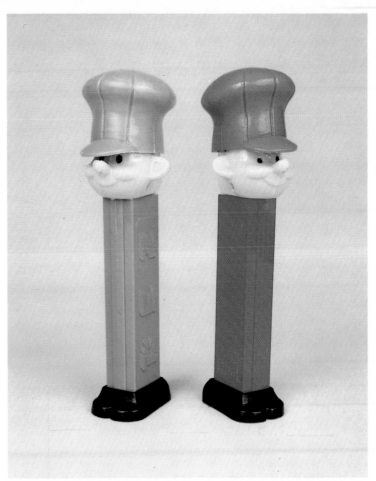

"Engineer" (PEZ® Pal), ca.
1970s, $30-50

"Maharajah" (PEZ® Pal), ca.
1960s, $20-30

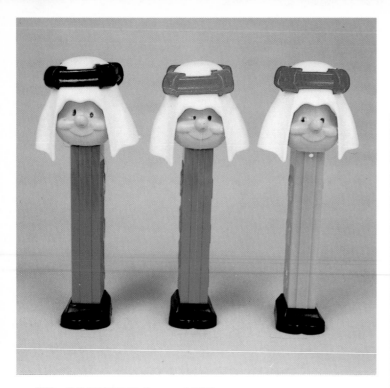

"Sheik" (PEZ® Pal), ca. 1960s,
$45-65

"Big Top Elephant (Flat Hat)",
ca. 1960s, Several color variations vary with the character.
$25-40

"Knight" (PEZ® Pal), ca. 1960s,
$100-125

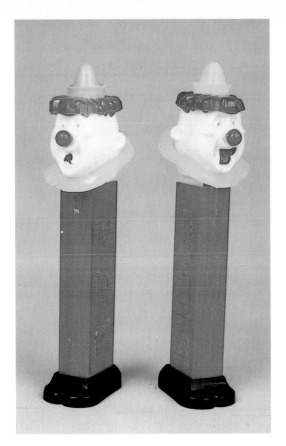

"Clown w/Collar", ca. 1960s,
$20-30

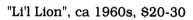"Li'l Lion", ca 1960s, $20-30

"Long Face Clown", ca. 1960s,
$20-30

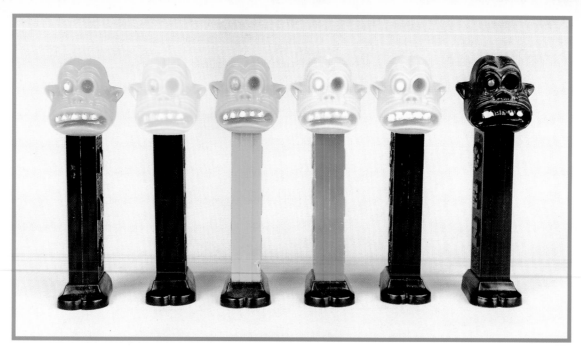

"One-Eye Monster", ca. 1960s,
$35-50

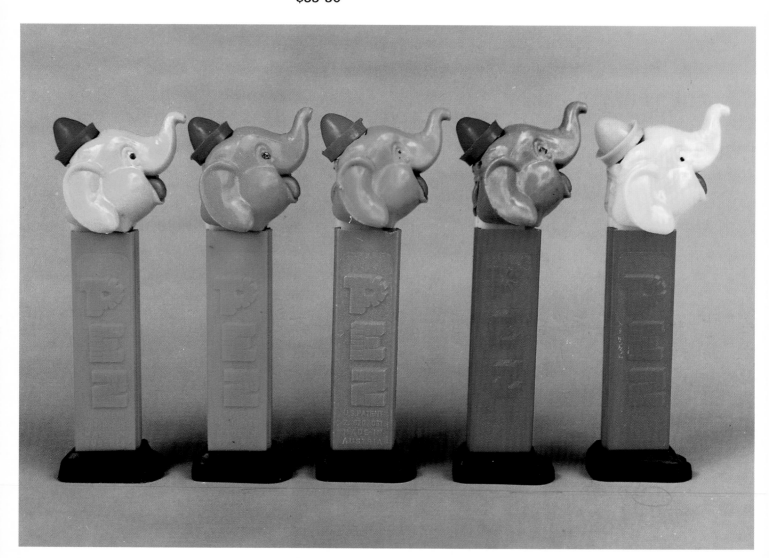

"Big Top Elephant (Point Hat)",
ca. 1960s, $30-45

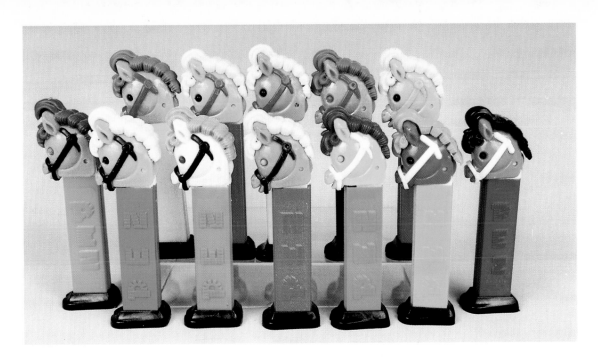

"Pony-Go-Round", ca. 1960s,
$25-40. Note: Some variations
in color may bring higher
prices.

"Big Top Elephant (with hair)",
ca. 1960s, $250-400

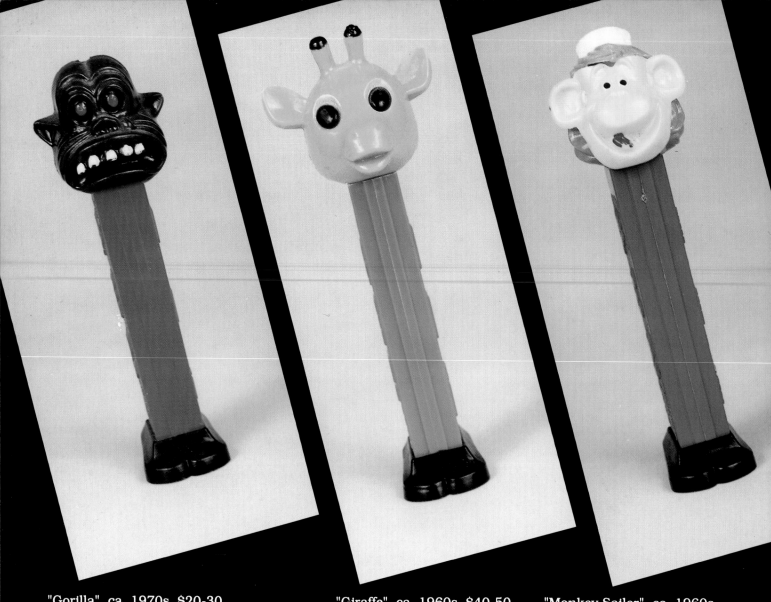

"Gorilla", ca. 1970s, $20-30

"Giraffe", ca. 1960s, $40-50

"Monkey Sailor", ca. 1960s, $20-30

"Cockatoo", ca. 1970s, $20-30

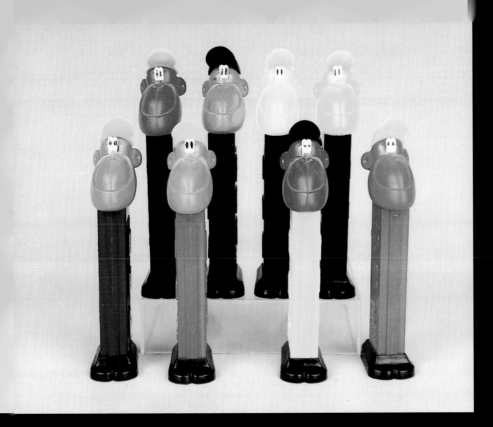

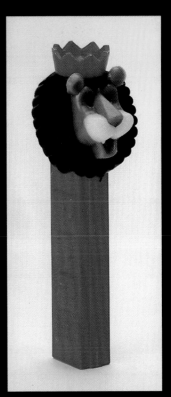

"Mimic the Monkey", ca.
1960s, $20-30

"Roar the Lion", ca. 1970s,
$35-50

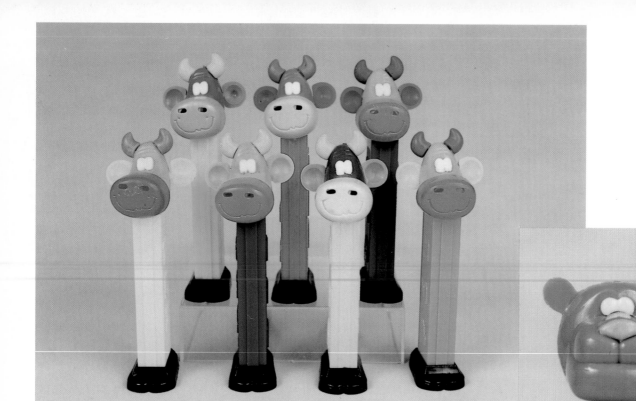

"Cow "B", ca. 1960s, $65-125

"Panther", ca. 1960s, $40-50

"Raven", ca. 1960s,
$20-30

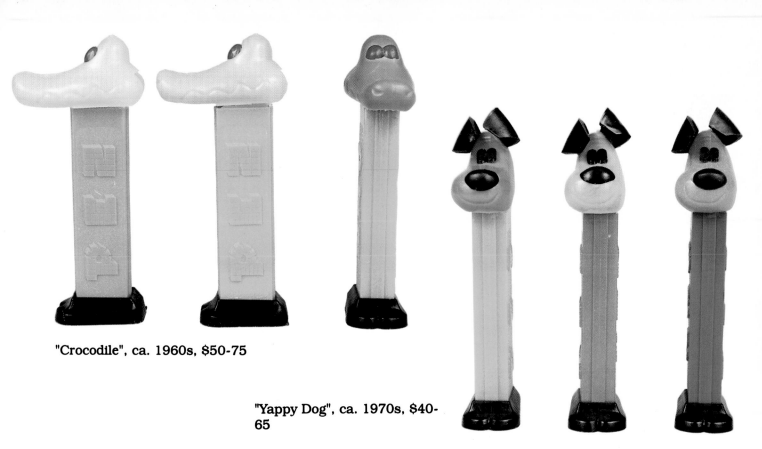

"Crocodile", ca. 1960s, $50-75

"Yappy Dog", ca. 1970s, $40-65

"Panda", ca. 1970s, white $10-20, yellow $75-125, red $250-350

43

"Cat w/Derby", ca. 1960s, $20-30

"Octopus", ca. 1960s, $30-50

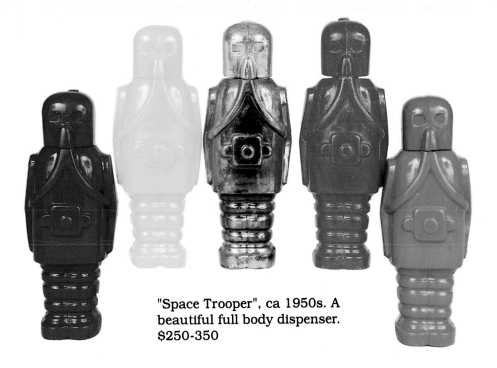

"Space Trooper", ca 1950s. A
beautiful full body dispenser.
$250-350

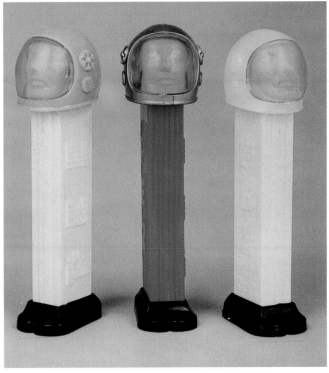

"Astronaut 1", ca. 1950s,
$150-200

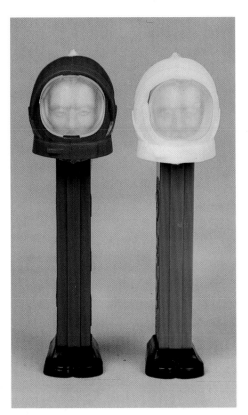

"Astronaut 2", ca. 1970s, $75-
100

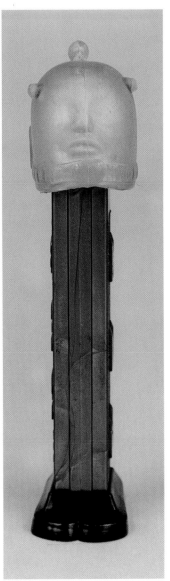

"Spaceman", ca 1950s, $100-
125

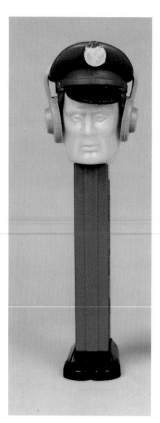

"Pilot", ca. 1970s, $50-75

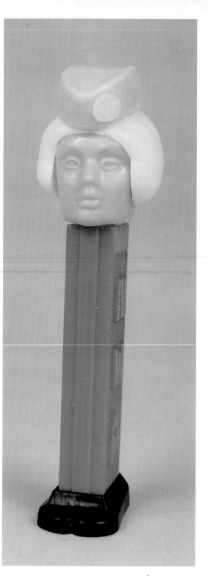

"Betsy Ross", ca. 1970s, $50-60

"Stewardess", ca. 1970s, $75- 100

"Uncle Sam", ca. 1970s, $50-75

"Captain", ca. 1970s, $50-60

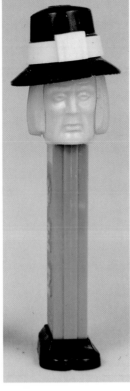

"Pilgrim", ca. 1970s, $75-100

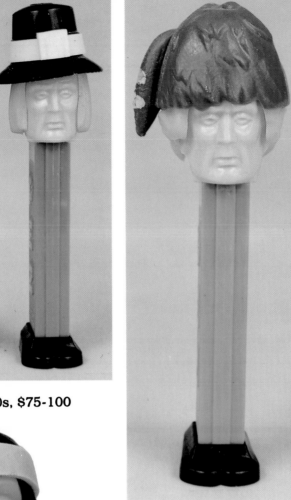

"Daniel Boone", ca. 1970s, $100-150

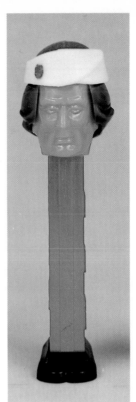

"Wounded Soldier", ca. 1970s, $75-100

"Indian Maiden", ca. 1970s, $50-75

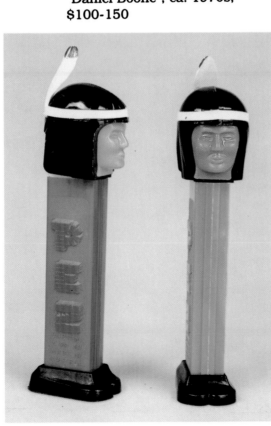

"Indian Brave", ca. 1970s, $150-200

"Cowboy", ca. 1960s, $200-300

"Indian Chief", ca. 1970s, $40-60

"Baseball Glove", ca. 1960s, $150-175, with Home Plate and Bat $150-300

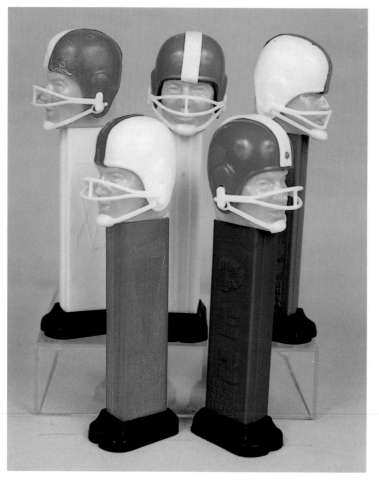

"Football Player", ca. 1960s, $85-125

"Camel Whistle", European issue. $10-20

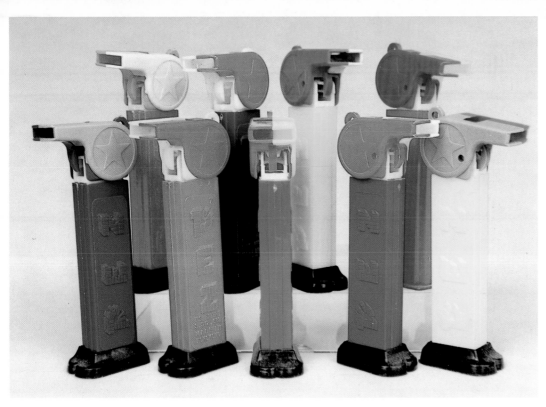

"Coach Whistle", ca. 1980s, $1-3

"Koala Whistle", European issue. $20-30

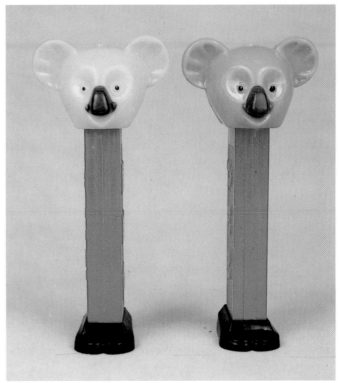

"Parrot, Rhino and Monkey Whistle", European issue. $1-5, Monkey $10-25

49

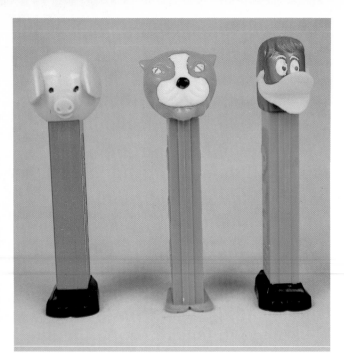

"Pig, Tiger and Duck Whistle",
European issue. $25-35, Tiger
$1-5

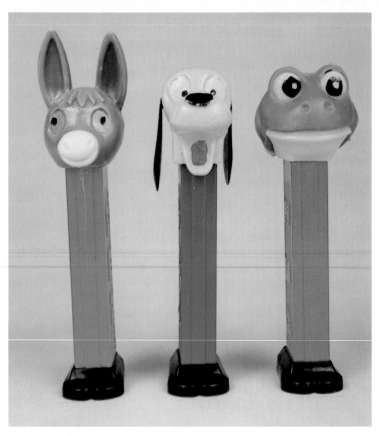

"Donkey, Dog and Frog
Whistle", European issue. $10-
40, Donkey $1-5

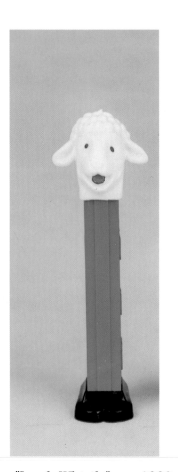

"Lamb Whistle", ca. 1980s,
$15-25

"Clown, Panda and Indian
Whistle", European issue. $1-5

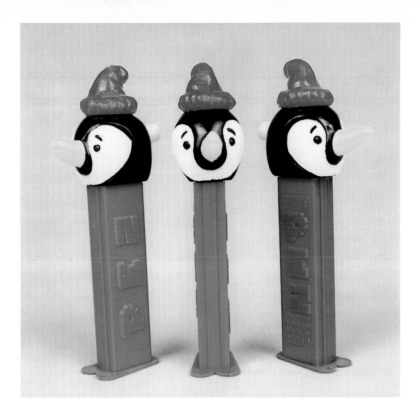

"Penguin Whistle", European
issue. Short $1-5, long $25-35

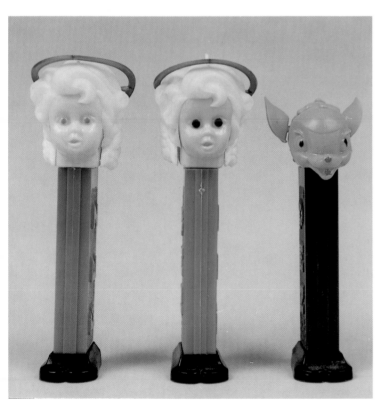

"Angel "A" and "B", Rudolph",
ca. 1980s, Angel "A" $5-15,
Angel "B" $25-50, Rudolph
$10-15

"Rooster Whistle", European
issue. $25-35

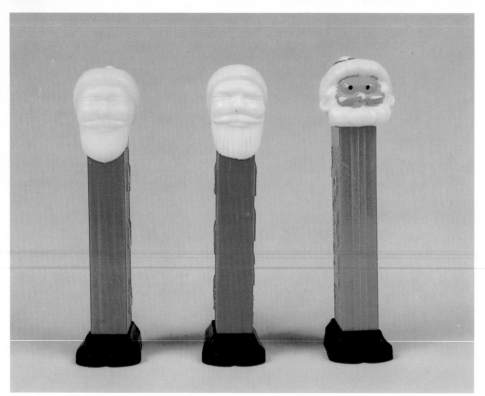

"Santa "A" and "B", Two earlier
versions of Kris Kringle. ca.
1950s, "A" $85-125, "B" $100-
150

"Full Body Santa Claus", A
beautiful figured dispenser. ca.
1950s, $100-150

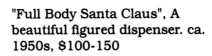

"Santa "C". A common dis-
penser. This has been made for
years. $1-3

"Snowman "A" and "B", This is
a very common dispenser. $1-3

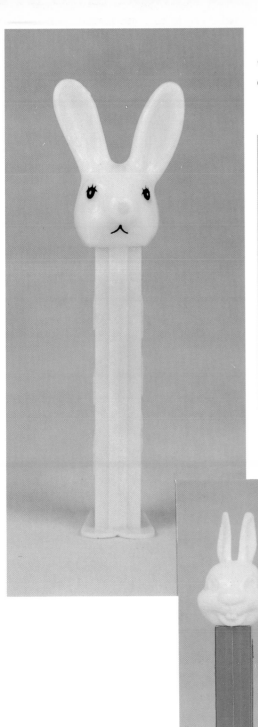

"Bunny", Revised. Current dispenser. $1-3

"Fat Ear Easter Bunny", A common dispenser. $1-5

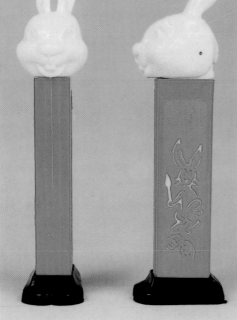

"Easter Bunny Die-Cut", A very rare dispenser. Beautifully designed. ca. 1950s, $350-500

"Easter Bunny "A", "B" and "C", These are very early versions of the Easter Rabbit. ca. 1960s, $300-350

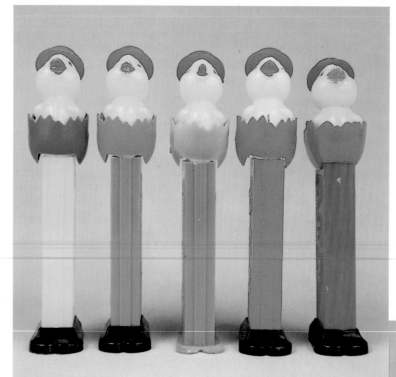

"Chick with Hat". A common dispenser. Different colored eggs are found. $1-5

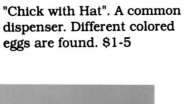

"Rooster", ca. 1970s, $20-30

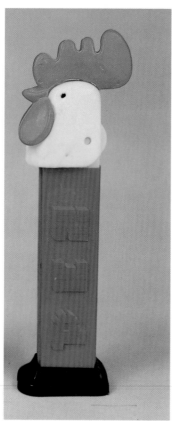

"Chick without Hat", ca. 1960s, $75-100

54

"Duck with Flower", ca. 1970s,
$25-35

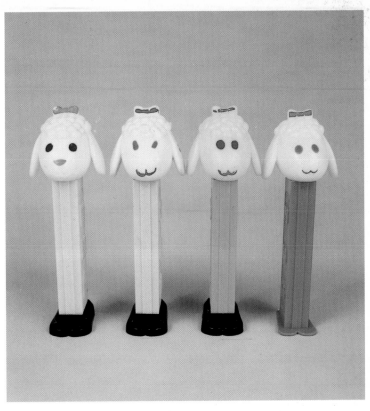

"Lamb". This dispenser is
readily available. $1-3

"3-Piece Witch "A". This can be
found in many different colors.
ca. 1970s, $10-20

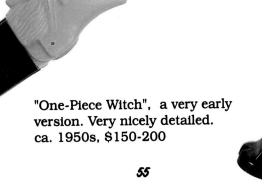

"One-Piece Witch", a very early
version. Very nicely detailed.
ca. 1950s, $150-200

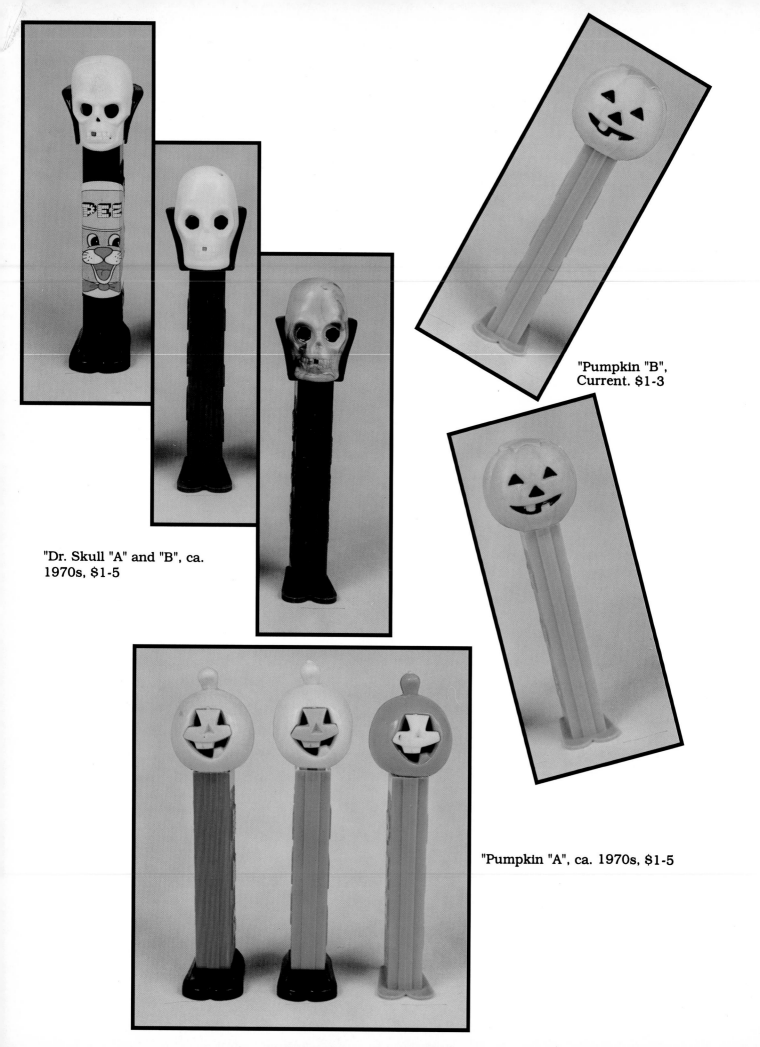

"Dr. Skull "A" and "B", ca. 1970s, $1-5

"Pumpkin "B", Current. $1-3

"Pumpkin "A", ca. 1970s, $1-5

"Eerie Spectres". These are rubber-headed dispensers. (Front row - left to right) Diabolic, Vamp, Zombie, Spook. (back row) Air Spirit and Scarewolf), ca. 1980s, $75-100

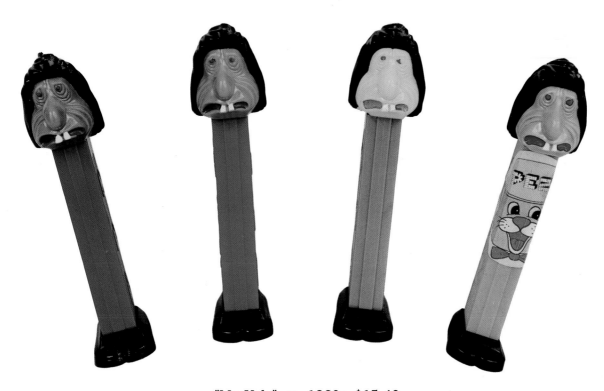

"Mr. Ugly", ca. 1960s, $15-40

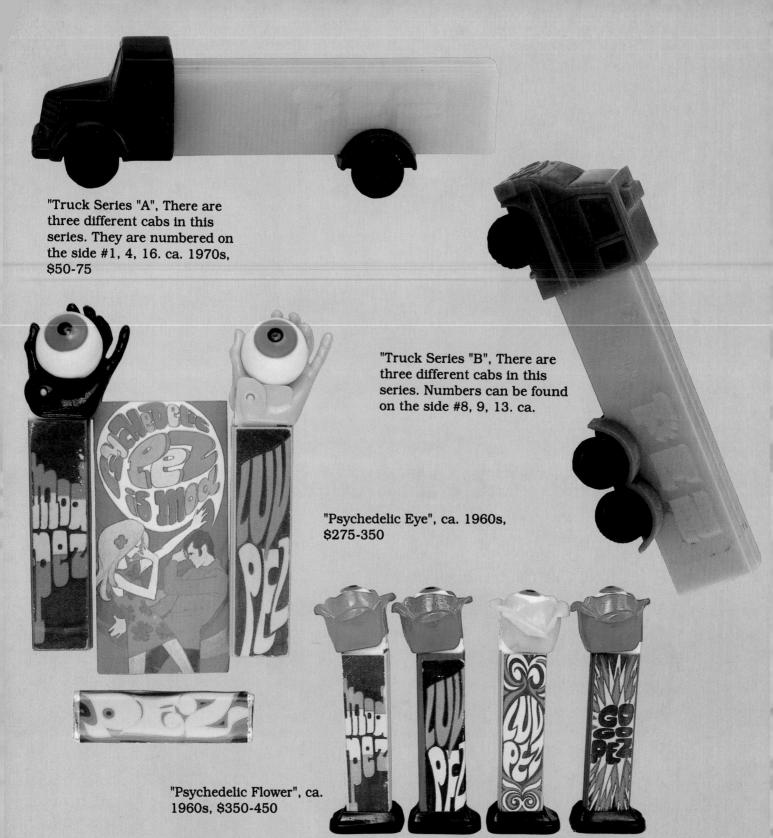

"Truck Series "A", There are three different cabs in this series. They are numbered on the side #1, 4, 16. ca. 1970s, $50-75

"Truck Series "B", There are three different cabs in this series. Numbers can be found on the side #8, 9, 13. ca.

"Psychedelic Eye", ca. 1960s, $275-350

"Psychedelic Flower", ca. 1960s, $350-450

"Truck Series "C", Ten different cabs were numbered #1-5, 16, R1-R4. Numbers are found on the side of the cab. $5-10

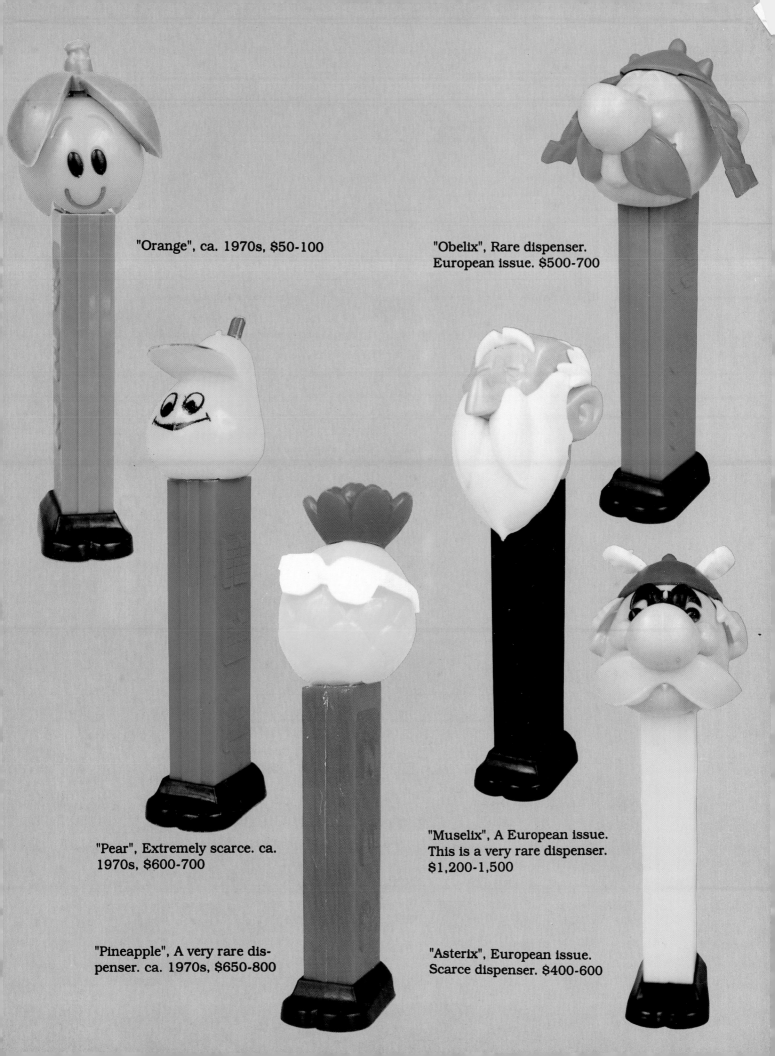

"Orange", ca. 1970s, $50-100

"Obelix", Rare dispenser. European issue. $500-700

"Pear", Extremely scarce. ca. 1970s, $600-700

"Muselix", A European issue. This is a very rare dispenser. $1,200-1,500

"Pineapple", A very rare dispenser. ca. 1970s, $650-800

"Asterix", European issue. Scarce dispenser. $400-600

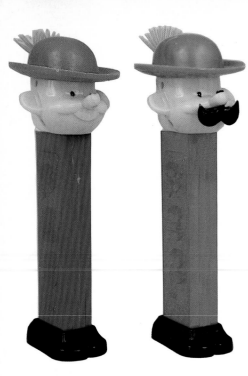

"Lion's Club Lion", Very rare.
ca. 1960s, $500-700

"Alpine Man", This dispenser is
from the '72 Olympics. ca.
1970s, $300-400

"Olympic Snowman", This is a
dispenser from the 1976
Olympics. $200-300

"Hippo", European issue.
Scarce. $400-450

"PIF", European issue. ca.
1980s, $75-100

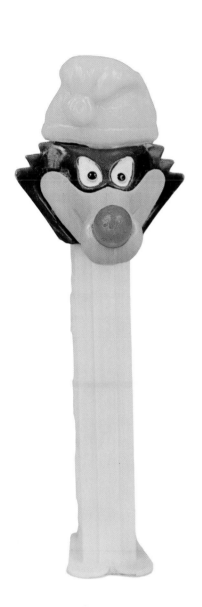

"Vucko Wolf", ca. 1980s, $400-500

"Vucko Wolf". From the 1984 Olympics. $400-500

"Sparefroh", A hard to find European issue. $200-300

"Vucko Wolf", ca. 1980s, $400-500

61

PEZ
Super
Spiel
158 lustige Gesichter

Doppel PEZ
Doppel PEZ
Doppel PEZ

Ein Steckkopf mit 15 Steckteilen

"Make-A-Face", This is an ultra rare dispenser made in the early 1970s. This is a Europcan issue. $1,500-3,000

98¢ fun to eat fun to shoot Ready-Aim-Fire! 98¢

CANDY PEZ SHOOTER DISPENSER

SEE BACK FOR EXCITING TARGET GAME

"Candy Shooter", ca. 1970s, $300-350

"'50s Space Gun", Bought at the store and available as a premium. This has great detail. $100-150

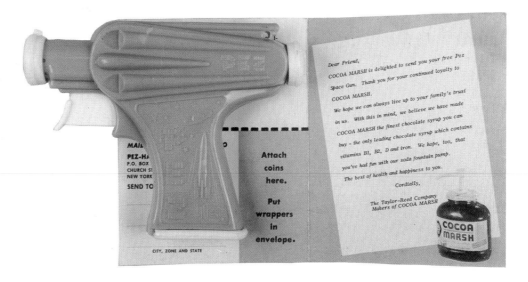

"Space Gun", Pulled from the market immediately making this a scarce item. ca. 1980s, $100-150

Chapter 2: Premiums

Through the years, kids were always encouraged to "save those wrappers" and send away for several different items.

New items continue to surface and collectors are finding these to be very exciting to own, and fun.

However, it is important to have the original paper work, and original packaging, to verify its authenticity, as some early premiums were not marked "PEZ®" Later years brought stickers, and tattoos and these are clearly marked.

"Cocoa Marsh". Available with chocolate syrup. ca. 1950s, $100-125

"Stand By Me". Came with a miniature poster from the movie. The dispenser has just a PEZ® Pal Boy. Must be MIB (Mint In Bag). ca. 1980s, $150-300

"PEZ® Yo-Yo.," ca. 1950s,
$275-350

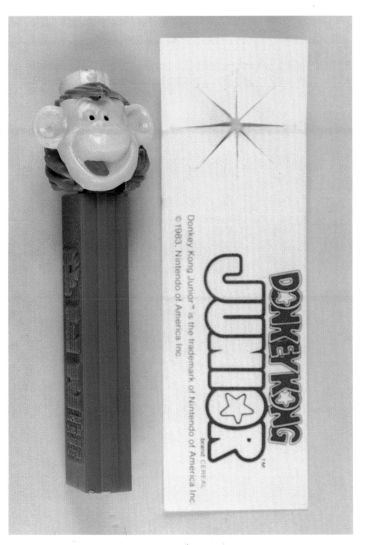

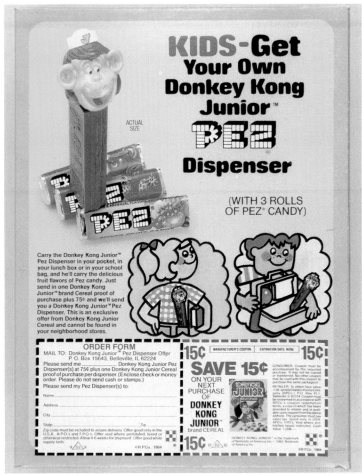

"Donkey Kong Jr.". Available
through a cereal promotion.
Has a yellow "J" on his cap.
Must have the letter on the cap
and paper insert, ca. 1980s,
$275-375

"Donkey Kong Jr." Cereal Box
offering premium. ca. 1980s,
$450-600

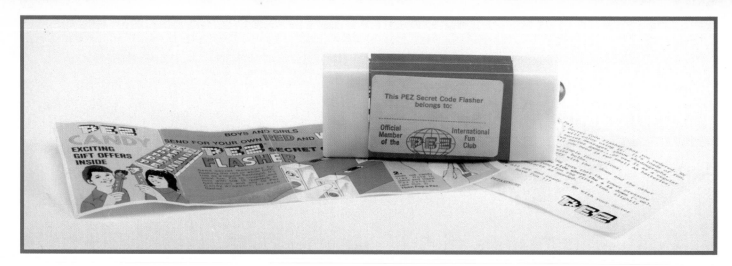

"Secret Code Flasher", A mail-
away with wrappers. ca.
1970s, $200-350, Very Rare

PEZ® Glasses", ca. 1970s,
$50-100

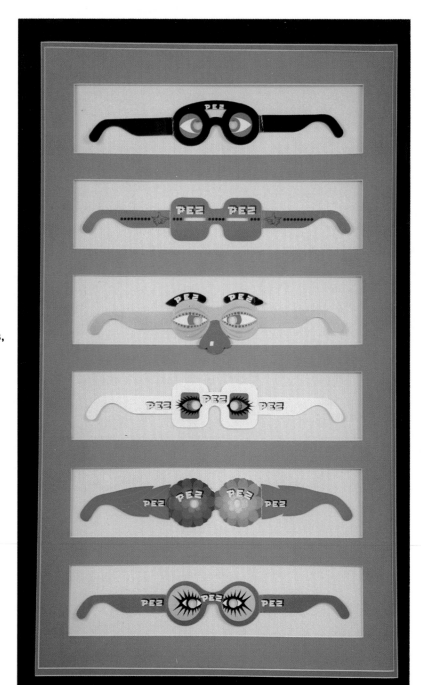

"Hobo Mask", ca. 1970s, $125-
175

"Ghoul Mask", ca. 1970s,
$250-300

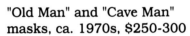

"Old Man" and "Cave Man"
masks, ca. 1970s, $250-300

"Spiderman" and "Hulk"
masks, ca. 1970s, $20-30

"Alpine Hat", ca. 1970s, $75-125

"Candy Pack Visor", ca. 1970s, $40-75

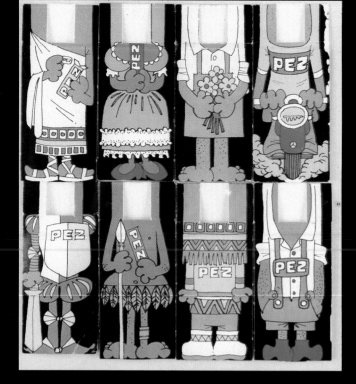

"Costumes "A"-series". These
costumes fit over the dispenser. ca. 1970s, $10-20

"Costume Book", ca. 1970s,
$150-250

"Costumes "B"-series". Used to
slide over the dispenser. ca.
1970s, $10-20

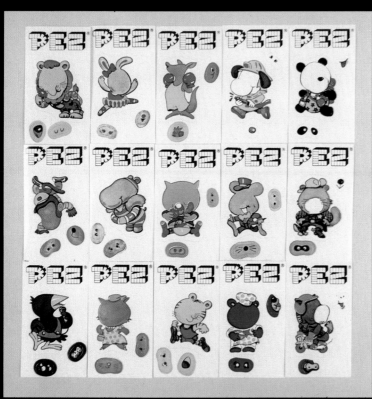

"PEZ® Stickers", ca. 1980s,
$10-25

"PEZ® Tattoos", ca. 1970s,
$10-20

"PEZ® Clickers", ca. 1970s,
$10-15

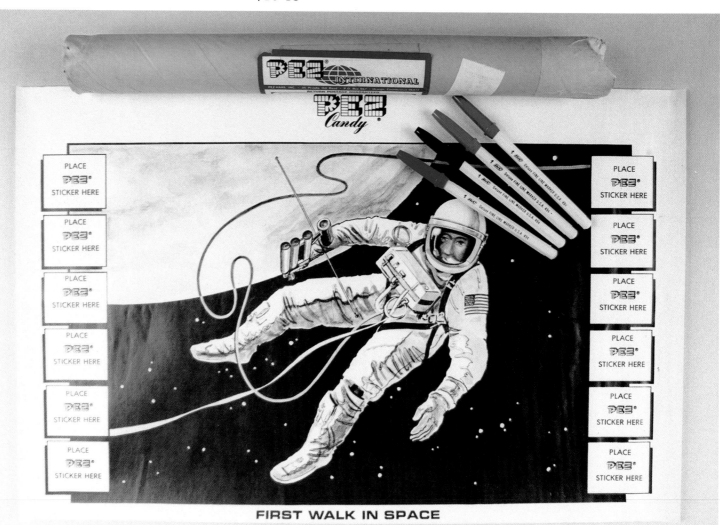

"Space Poster", ca. 1970s,
$150-250

"PEZ® Sticker-Doubles", ca. 1970s, $15-30

"PEZ® Coin Holder", ca. 1970s, $50-125

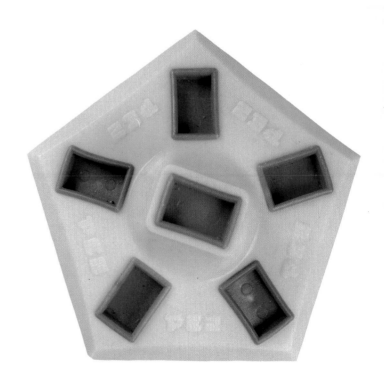

"Pentagon Stand", Used to hold 6 dispensers. ca. 1960s, $100-150

"PEZ® Holiday Dish", ca.
1950s, $150-225

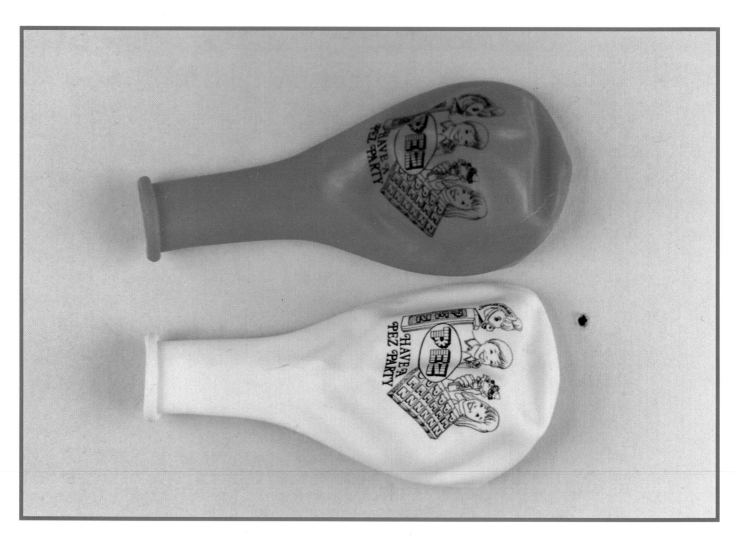

"PEZ® Balloons", ca. 1970s,
$10-20

"Captain Nord Story Book", ca. 1950s, $1,000-1,500 *Courtesy of S. Luksenburg*

"PEZ® Box Insert", ca. 1950s, $100-200

"White Castle© Ceiling Ad". Used as a Halloween promotion. ca. 1990s, $125-200

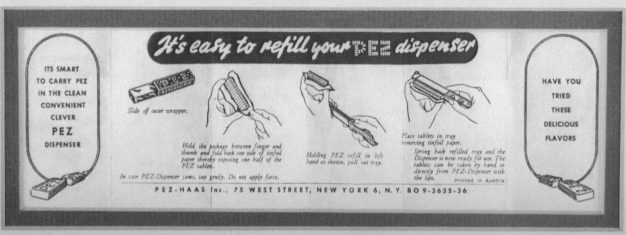

"Refill Insert". This insert
explained how to load a dispenser. ca. 1950s, $100-200

HOW TO WIN A GOLDEN PEZ DISPENSER

1. Print your name and address on reverse side.

2. Tear off coupon and mail together with 25 PEZ wrappers (any flavor will do) to:

**PEZ-HAAS, INC.
75 West Street
New York 6, N. Y.**

Printed in Austria

An exciting gift for kids and adults alike

Is Yours for 25 PEZ Wrappers

Dispenser

A Beautiful Golden

Free!

TRY ALL SIX DELICIOUS

FLAVORS

- Peppermint
- Wild Cherry
- Orange
- Lemon
- Lime
- Anise

How To Refill Your Dispenser

1. Slide off outer wrapper. SAVE FOR FREE GOLDEN DISPENSER.

2. Hold package between index finger and thumb. Fold back foil paper to expose one half of PEZ tablets.

3. Hold refill in one hand. Pull out Santa's head with other hand. Place tablets into tray, pull out foil, and slide tray back. Press down pompon of Santa's cap and out pops your PEZ.

If tray jams, slide it back and forth a few times. Do not use force.

Tear off here

CX 1000—755

City

Zone

Street

State

Name

Enclose your 25 PEZ wrappers with this coupon and mail to:

PEZ-HAAS, INC.—75 West St., New York 6, N.Y.

[PLEASE PRINT]

"PEZ® Insert", Used with wrappers and $.25 to receive "Golden Glow" dispenser. ca. 1950s, $100-200

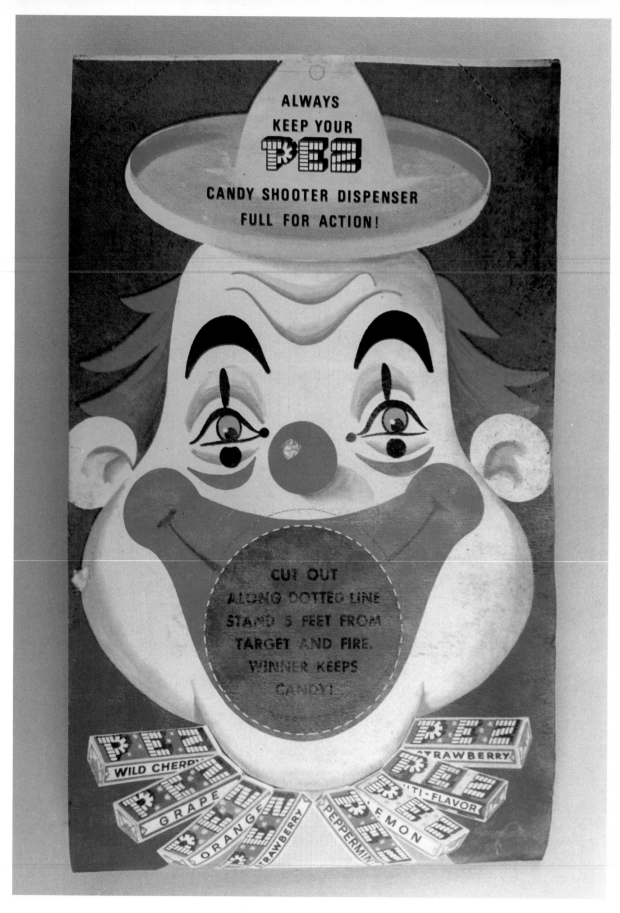

"Candy Shooter Target". A neat
looking item used to shoot at.
ca. 1970s, $75-100

"PEZ® Pirate T-Shirt", A mail-
away with wrappers. ca.
1960s, $75-125

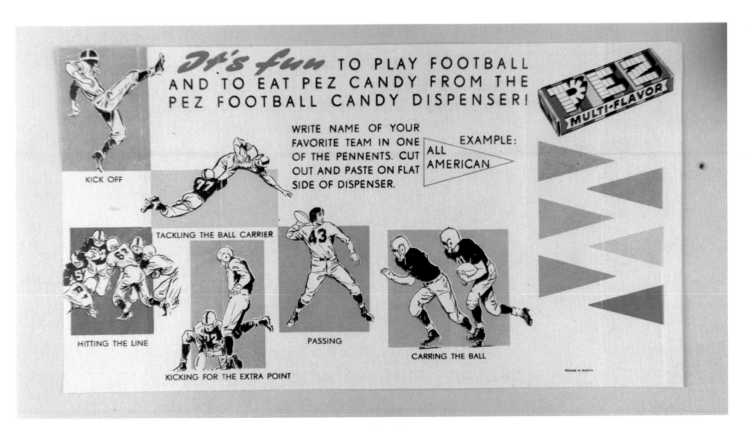

"Football Insert". This insert
was used to place a pennant
on the side of the Football
Player. ca. 1960s, $45-75

"Pezi Comic Strip", Enclosed
with dispenser and candy. Pezi
changed into many disguises.
A whole series of Pezi dispensers were made. ca. 1970s, $50-
80

"Candy Shooter Insert", Also
available was the Jumbo Jot
Pen. ca. 1970s, $50-80

"Arithmetic and Golden Glow
Insert", ca. 1960s, $100-200

"PEZ® Candy Shooter Insert",
ca. 1960s, $60-120

"Popeye© Comic Insert", ca.
1960s, $100-200

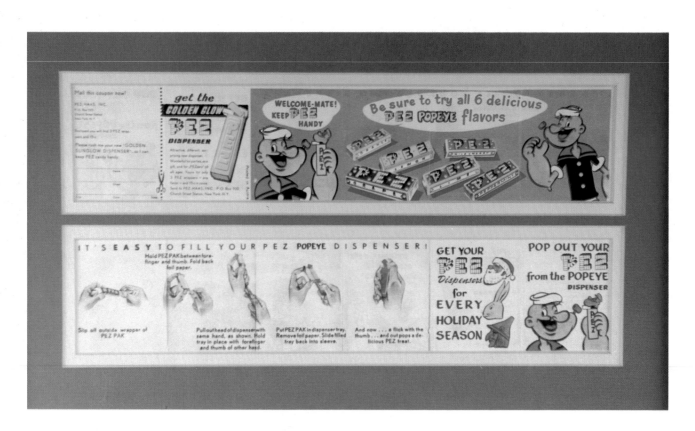

"Popeye© and Golden Glow
Insert", ca. 1950s, $75-150

"Costumes and Golden Glow
Insert", ca. 1970s, $35-60

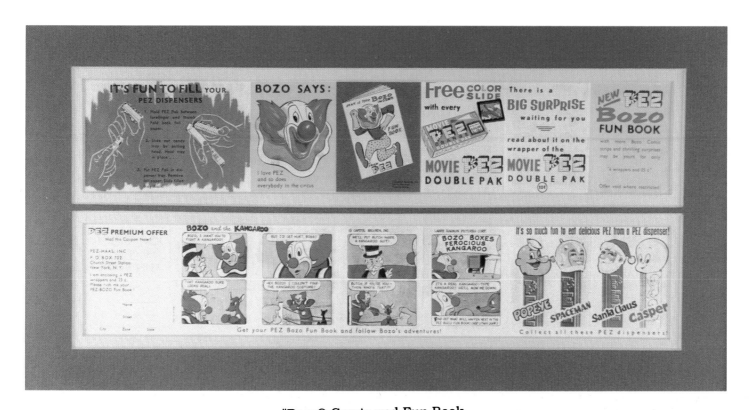

"Bozo© Comic and Fun Book
Insert", Also available with
wrappers and $.25 was the
PEZ® movie pak. ca. 1960s,
$100-200

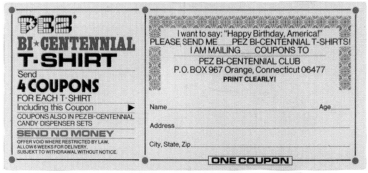

"Bi-Centennial Insert", Used to
send away for the "Happy
Birthday, America" T-shirt. ca.
1970s, $35-60

"Spiderman and Hulk Mask
Insert", ca. 1970s, $10-20

Chapter 3: Store Displays

So much history can be learned from display items. The type of characters or items that were available. The artwork and color of many of these items are wonderful, and can enhance anyone's collection.

There have been several different types of displays. Floor displays are very prominent in grocery stores, along with vending machines. There are also counter boxes, racks and displays.

Many older displays are still being found and it helps to put answers to questions and continues to solve puzzles regarding PEZ® dispensers.

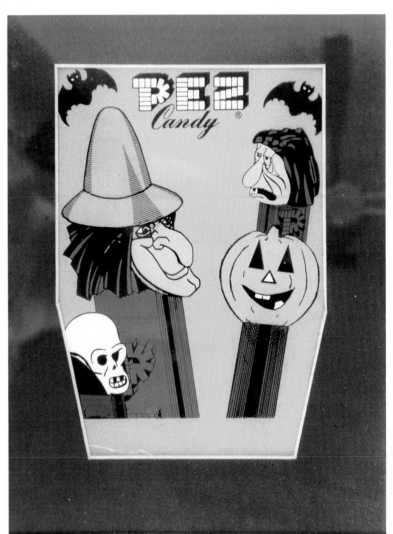

"Halloween Header", ca. 1970s, $150-225

"Soft-Headed Super Hero's
Header", ca. 1970s, $300-500

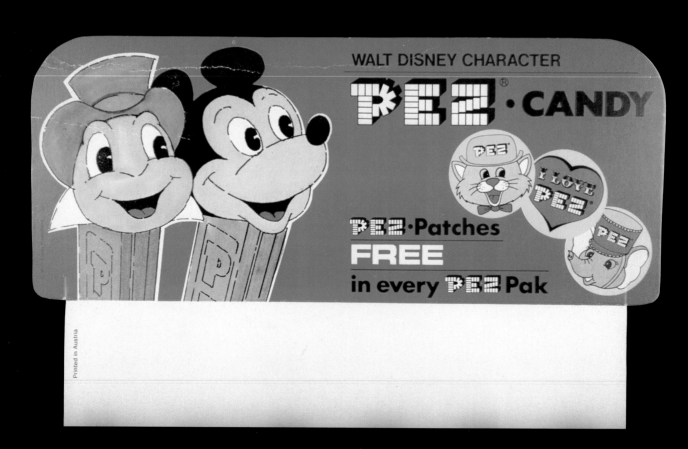

"Disney© WDP Header", ca.
1960s, $150-225

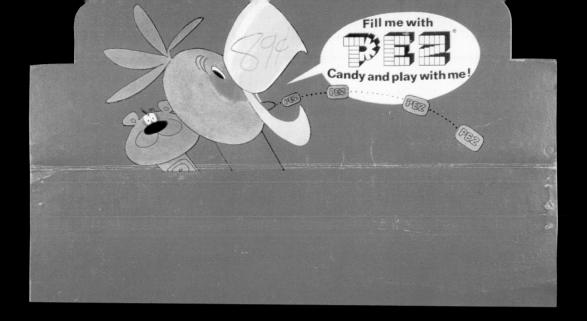

"Kooky Zoo Header", ca. 1970s,
$100-175

"Warner Brothers© Header",
ca. 1980s, $150-225

"PEZ® Pal Header", ca. 1960s,
$175-350 *Courtesy of J.
Kilgour*

"PEZ® Pal Header", ca. 1970s,
$100-150

"Bi-Centennial Header", ca.
1970s, $250-375

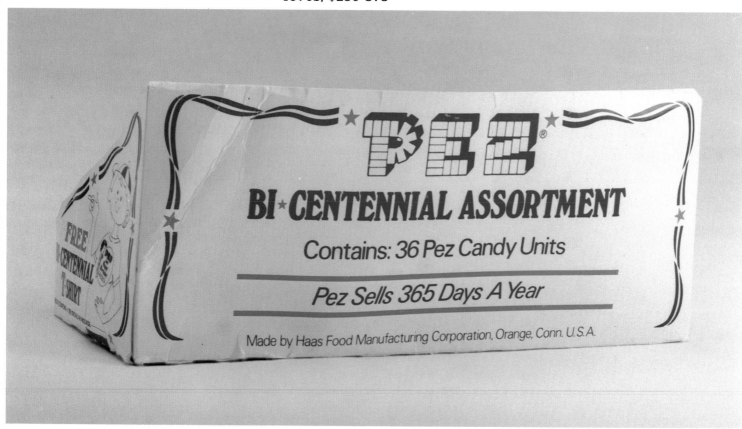

"Bi-Centennial Counter Box",
ca. 1970s, $250-375 *Courtesy
J. Kilgour*

© 1965 Universal Pictures Co., Inc.

CREATURE
PEZ CANDY DISPENSER SET

Indian Chief
PEZ CANDY DISPENSER SET

Circus Horse
PEZ CANDY DISPENSER SET

Peter Pan
PEZ CANDY DISPENSER SET

OCTOPUS
PEZ CANDY DISPENSER SET

POPEYE
PEZ CANDY DISPENSER SET

"Vending Boxes", ca. 1960s, $45-200 (Depending on Character)

"Vending boxes", ca. 1970s, $15-40

"50s Spacegun Display" ca.
1950s, $300-375

"Various Headers", ca. 1980s,
$5-15

"Popeye© Counter Box", ca. 1960s, $450-750

"Green Hornet© Counter Box", ca. 1960s, $350-500

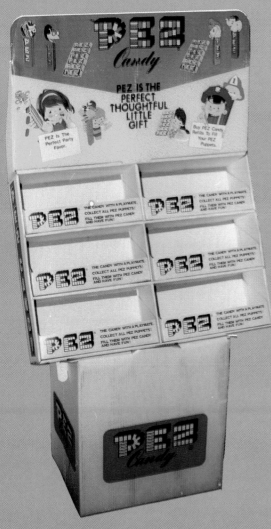

"Floor Display", 24" x 50", ca. 1970s, $100-150

"Peter PEZ® Counter Display", ca. 1990s, $25-50

"Disney© WDP Counter Top Display", ca. 1960s, $400-650

"Santa Display Box", ca.
1950s, $200-350

"Disney© WDP Counter Box",
ca. 1970s, $200-325

"Universal Monster© Counter
Box", ca. 1960s, $350-500

"Super Hero's Counter Box",
ca. 1970s, $225-325

"Football Player Counter Box",
ca. 1960s, $300-400

"Anise Counter Box", ca.
1940s, $500-750

"Candy Counter Box", ca.
1970s, $150-200

"Six-Pack Candy Box", ca.
1970s, $135-190

"Disney© WDP Blister Card",
ca. 1970s, $30-40

"Hulk© Blister Card", ca. 1970s, $25-35

"Disney© WDP Blister Card", ca. 1980s, $30-40

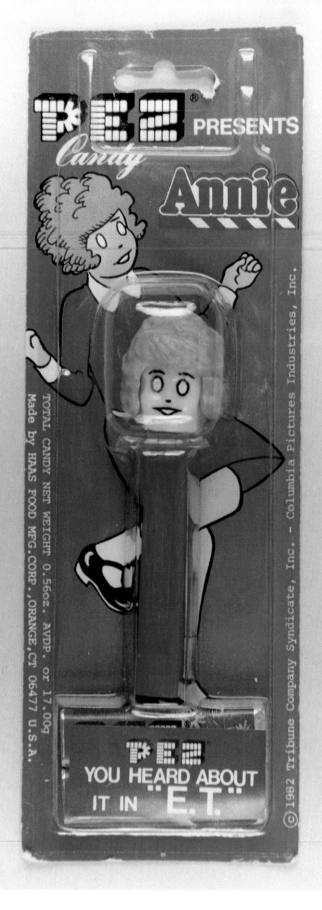

"Smurf© Blister Card", ca.
1980s, $10-15

"Annie© Blister Card", ca.
1980s, $80-150

"Halloween Blister Card", ca.
1980s, $60-125

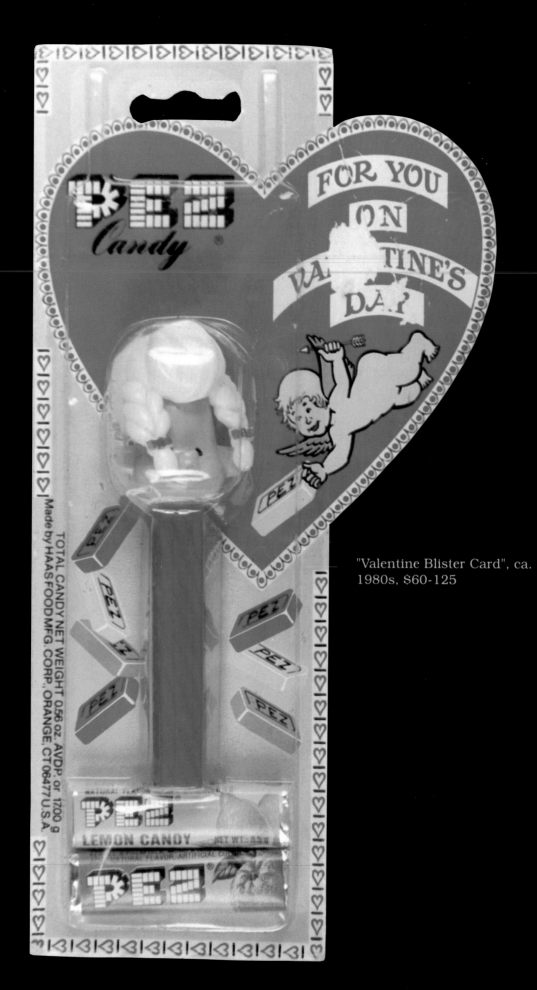

"Valentine Blister Card", ca.
1980s, $60-125

Index